101 Terrific Tiki Designs for Coloring

Scott Cummins

OUTSIDE-THE-LINES.COM

OUTSIDE-THE-LINES.com

OUTSIDE-THE-LINES.COM

OUTSIDE-THE-LINES.COM

OUTSIDE-THE-LINES.COM

OUTSIDE-THE-LINES.COM

OUTSIDE-THE-LINES.COM

OUTSIDE-THE-LINES.COM

OUTSIDE-THE-LINES.COM

OUTSIDE-THE-LINES.COM

OUTSIDE-THE-LINES.COM

OUTSIDE-THE-LINES.COM

OUTSIDE-THE-LINES.COM

OUTSIDE-THE-LINES.com

OUTSIDE-THE-LINES.COM

OUTSIDE-THE-LINES.COM

OUTSIDE-THE-LINES.COM

OUTSIDE-THE-LINES.COM

OUTSIDE-THE-LINES.COM

OUTSIDE-THE-LINES.COM

OUTSIDE-THE-LINES.COM

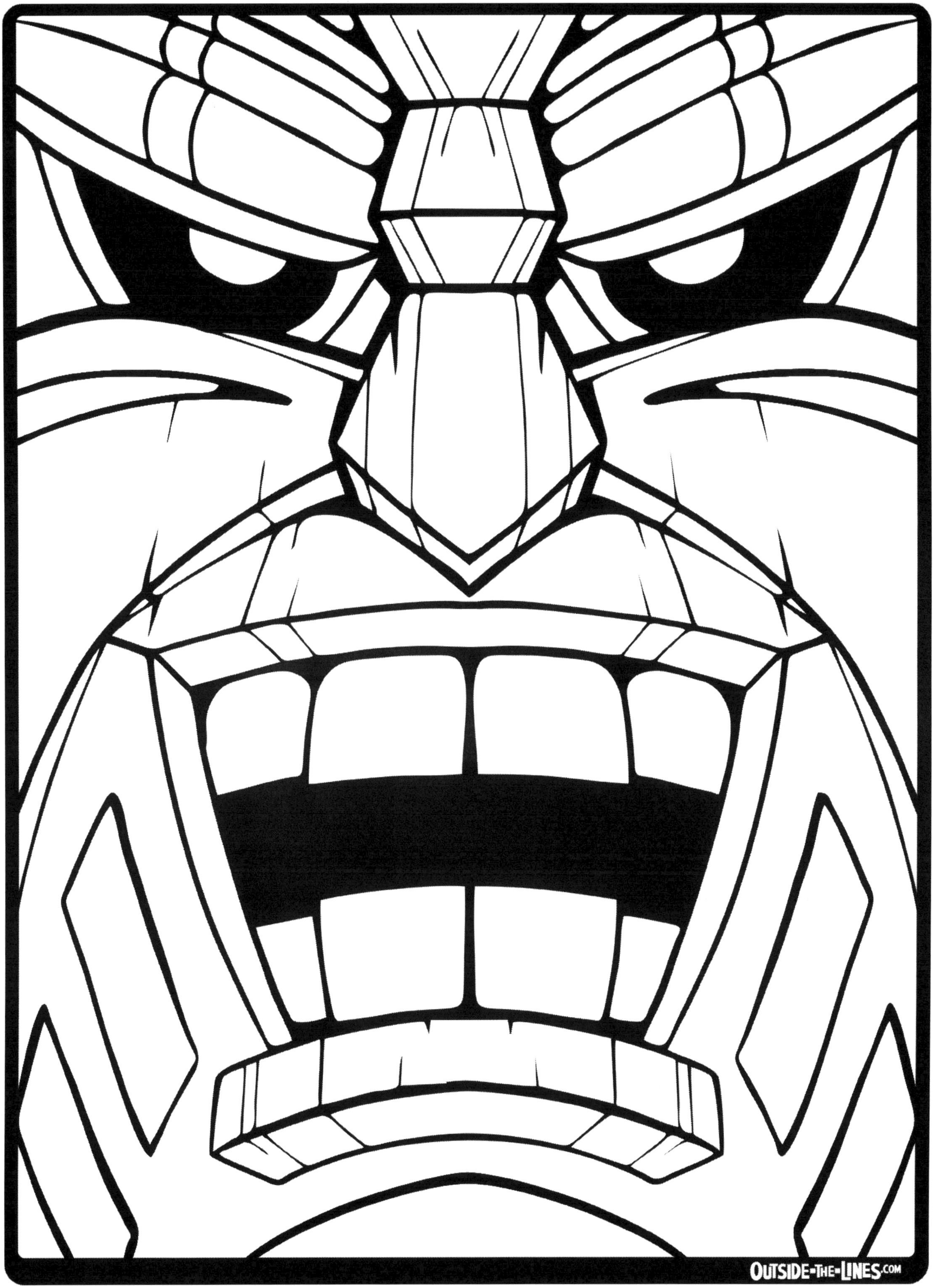
OUTSIDE-THE-LINES.COM

OUTSIDE-THE-LINES.COM

OUTSIDE-THE-LINES.COM

OUTSIDE-THE-LINES.COM

OUTSIDE-THE-LINES.COM

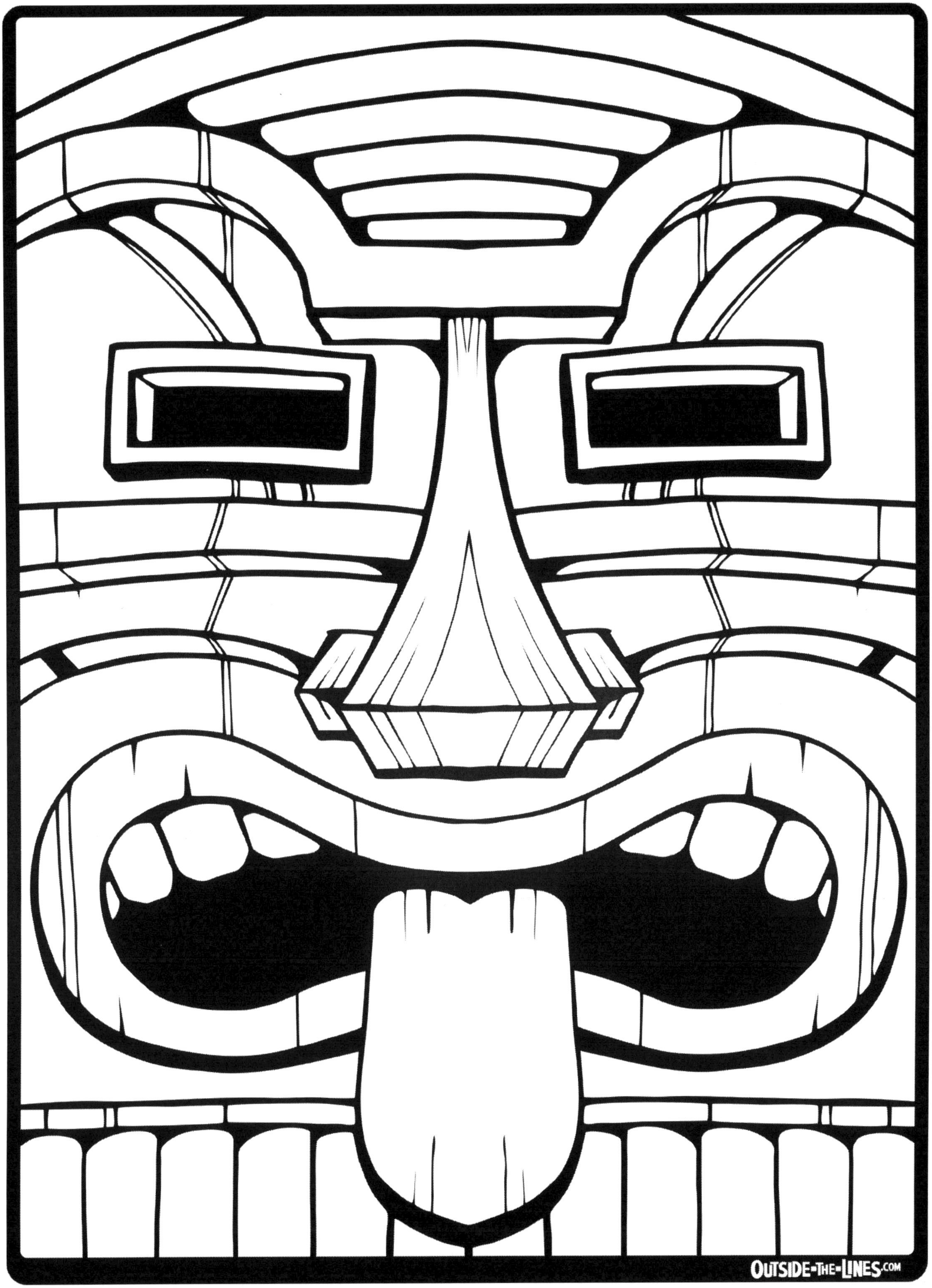

OUTSIDE-THE-LINES.COM

OUTSIDE-THE-LINES.COM

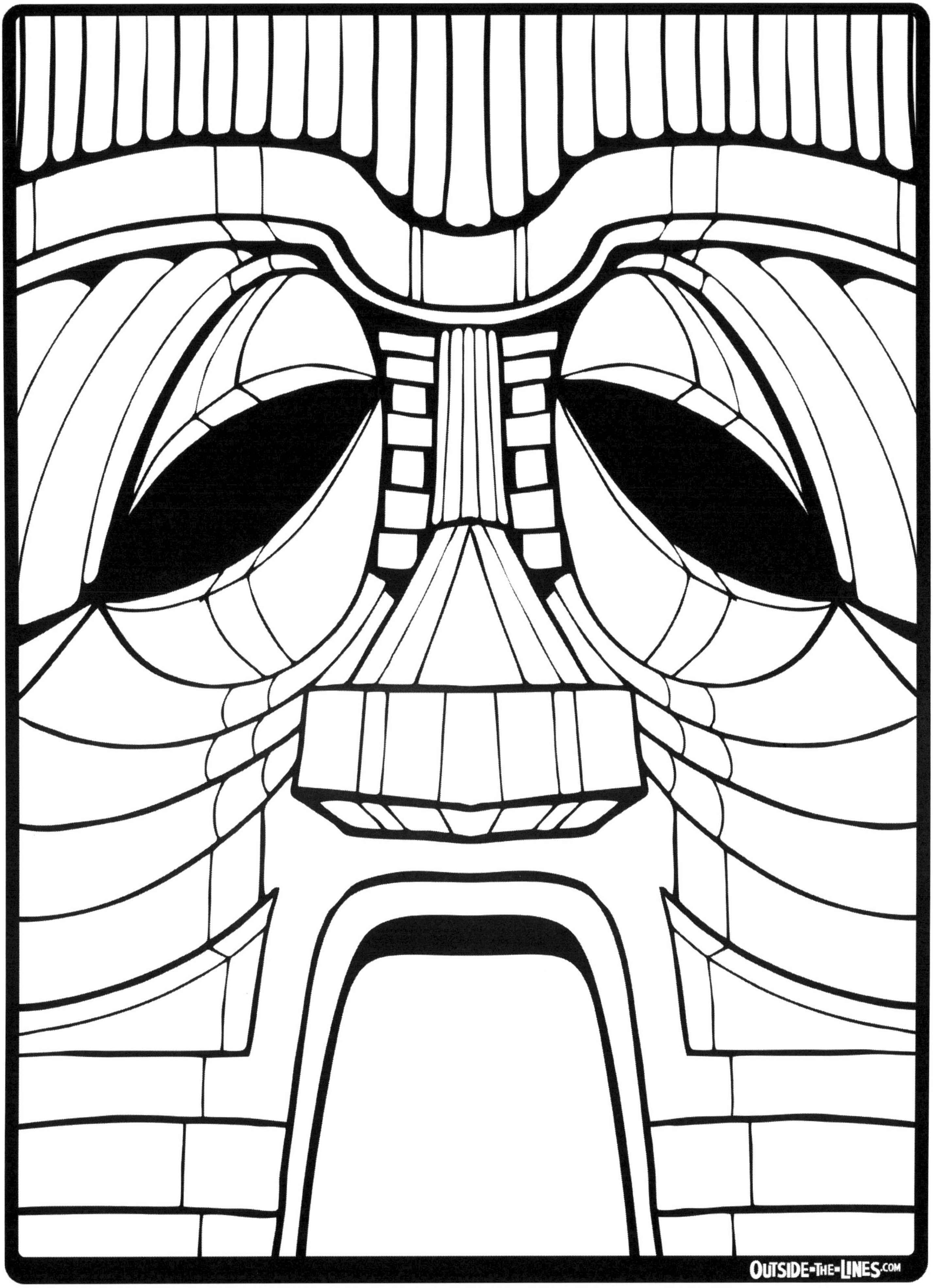
OUTSIDE-THE-LINES.COM

OUTSIDE-THE-LINES.COM

OUTSIDE-THE-LINES.COM

OUTSIDE-THE-LINES.COM

OUTSIDE-THE-LINES.COM

OUTSIDE-THE-LINES.COM

OUTSIDE-THE-LINES.com

OUTSIDE-THE-LINES.COM

OUTSIDE-THE-LINES.com

OUTSIDE-THE-LINES.com

OUTSIDE-THE-LINES.COM

OUTSIDE-THE-LINES.com

OUTSIDE-THE-LINES.com

OUTSIDE-THE-LINES.COM

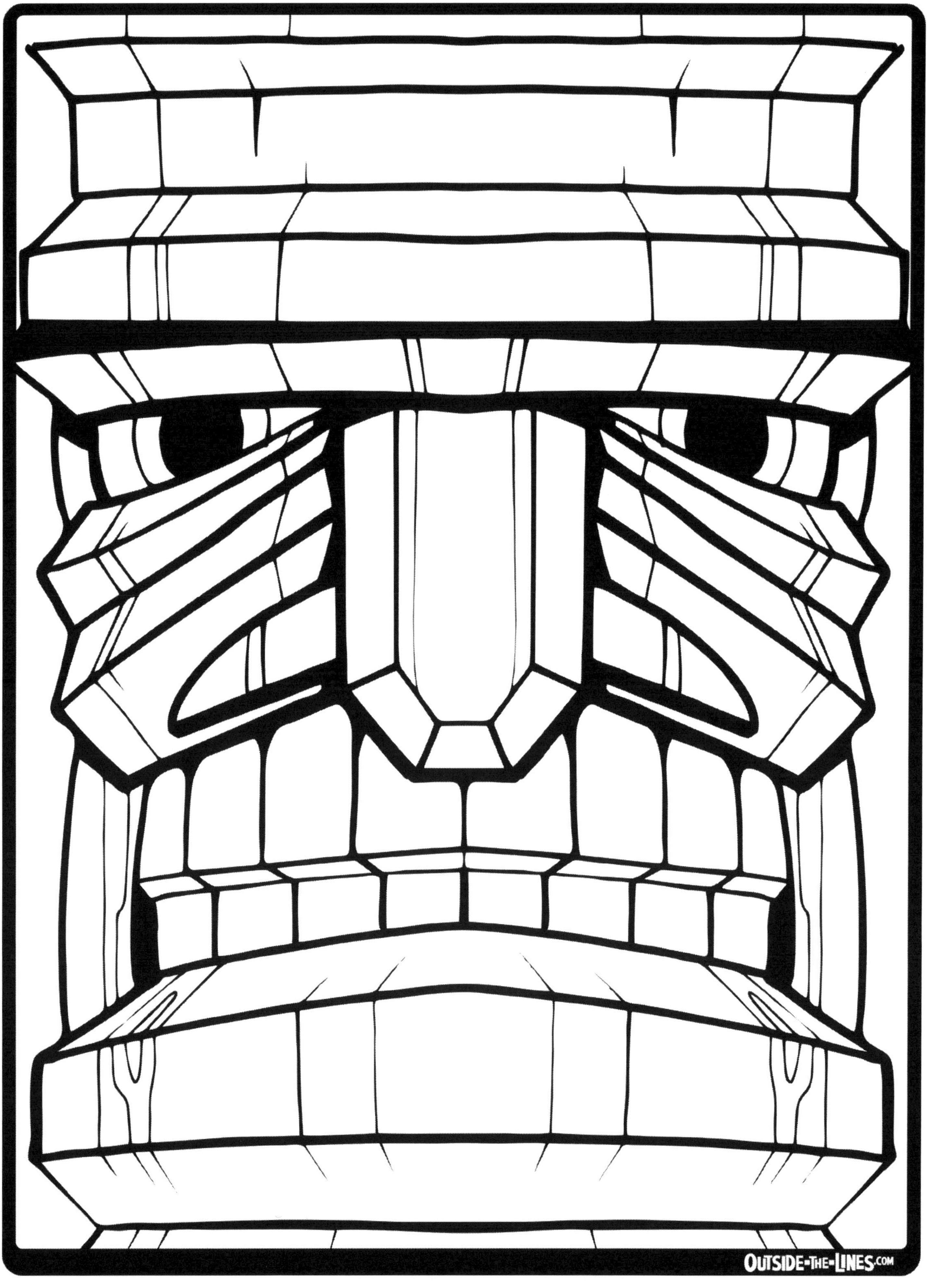

OUTSIDE-THE-LINES.COM

OUTSIDE-THE-LINES.COM

OUTSIDE-THE-LINES.COM

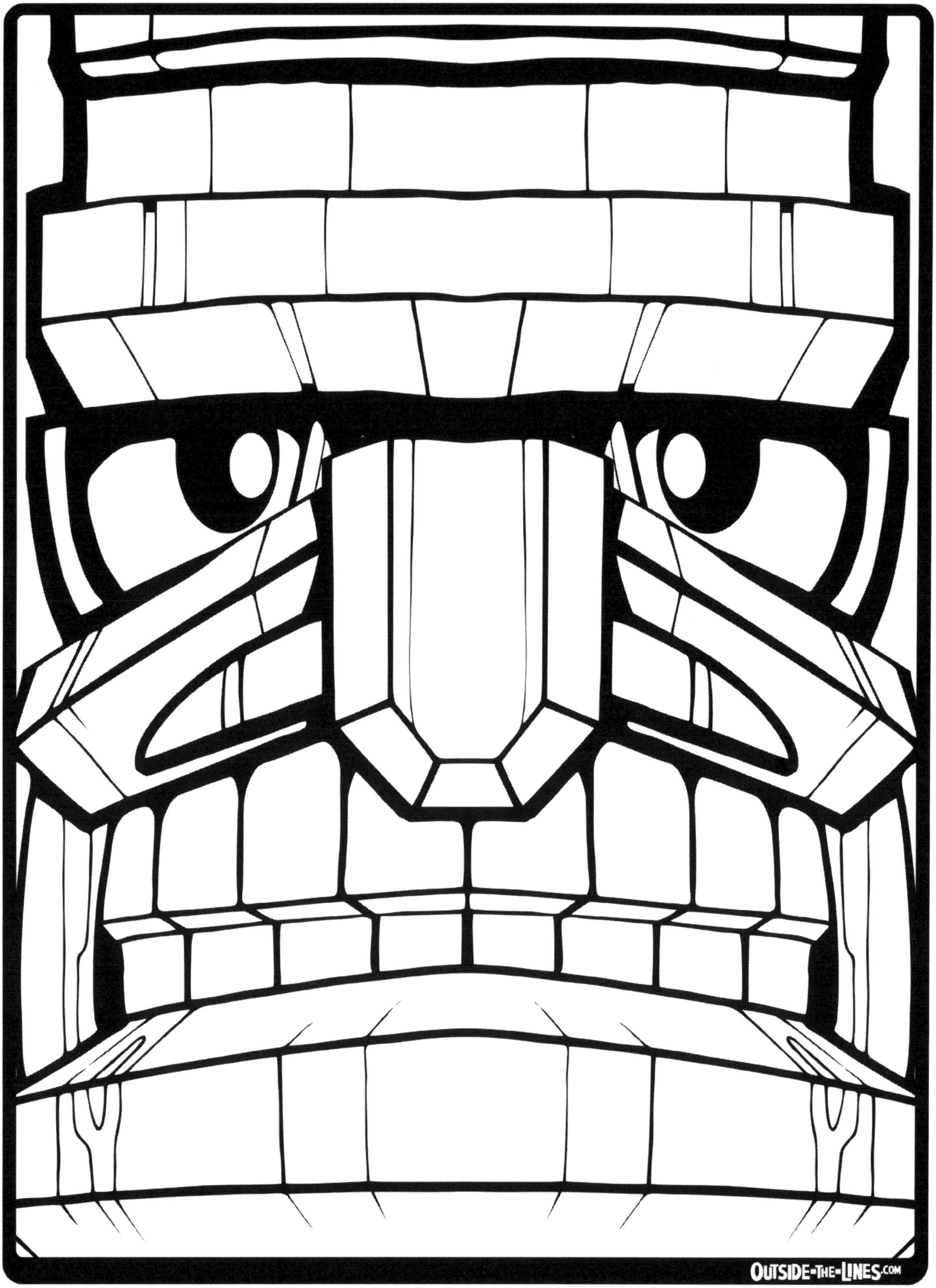

OUTSIDE-THE-LINES.COM

OUTSIDE-THE-LINES.COM

OUTSIDE-THE-LINES.COM

OUTSIDE-THE-LINES.COM

OUTSIDE-THE-LINES.COM

OUTSIDE-THE-LINES.COM

76768379R00115

Made in the USA
San Bernardino, CA
15 May 2018